THIS WAY, DELIGHT

The editor of this anthology of poetry for the young is a distinguished poet, writer, and critic. As the title indicates, he has chosen as keynote for his selection the word "delight." His aim is to introduce young readers to poetry whose inspiration is within the realm of their experience—which is not necessarily poetry written especially for children.

The range of selection is wide: the Elizabethan poets stand next to Emily Dickinson, Tennyson, Kipling, and to such moderns as Yeats, Wallace Stevens, e.e. cummings, Gerard Manley Hopkins, T. S. Eliot, Dylan Thomas. The grouping in five sections—Charms—Songs—Enchantments—Escapes—Stories—leads gradually from the simpler poems to the more difficult. *This Way, Delight* is not addressed to a particular age group. It is meant as a book to grow with, as a place in which to discover, as time goes by, new joys and new delights.

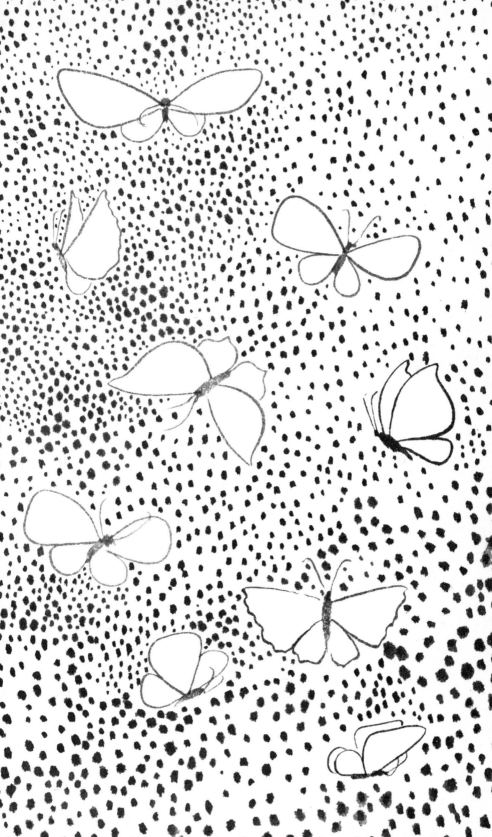

THIS WAY, DELIGHT

a
book
of   *selected by*   **Herbert Read**
poetry   *illustrated by* **Juliet Kepes**
for
the young

PANTHEON

My thanks are due to the authors, or their representatives, and to the publishers concerned, for permission to include copyright poems from the following sources: George Allen & Unwin, Ltd., "In Glencullen" from *Poems* by John M. Synge. Appleton-Century-Crofts, Inc., "The Flower-Fed Buffaloes" from *Going-to-the-Stars* by Vachel Lindsay. Copyright, 1926, D. Appleton & Company. Reprinted by permission of the publishers Appleton-Century-Crofts, Inc. Brandt & Brandt, "All in green went my love riding," "In Just-spring," "Lady will you come with me into" from *Poems 1923-1954*, Harcourt, Brace and Company. Copyright, 1923, 1931, 1951 by E. E. Cummings. Burns, Oates & Washbourne, "To a Snowflake" from *Collected Poems* by Francis Thompson. Doubleday and Company, Inc., "The Way through the Woods" from *Rewards and Fairies*, by Rudyard Kipling. Copyright 1910 by Rudyard Kipling, reprinted by permission of Mrs. George Bambridge and Doubleday and Company, Inc. Harcourt, Brace and Company, Inc., "Cape Ann" and "New Hampshire" from *Collected Poems 1909-1935* by T. S. Eliot. Copyright, 1936, by Harcourt, Brace and Company, Inc. Henry Holt and Company, Inc., "All That's Past," "The Listeners," "Nod," from *Collected Poems* by Walter de la Mare. Copyright, 1920, by Henry Holt and Company, Inc. Copyright, 1948, by Walter de la Mare, reprinted by permission of the publishers; "Stopping by Woods on a Snowy Evening," from *Complete Poems of Robert Frost*. Copyright, 1930, 1949, by Henry Holt and Company, Inc., New York, N.Y., reprinted by permission of the publishers. Mr. Richard Hughes and Chatto & Windus, Ltd., "Explanation, on Coming Home Late," "Old Cat Care," "Winter" from *Confessio Juvenis* by Richard Hughes. Alfred A. Knopf, Inc., "Janet Waking" from *Selected Poems* by John Crowe Ransom. Copyright 1927, 1945 by Alfred A. Knopf, Inc.; "Ploughing on Sunday" and "Earthy Anecdote" from *The Collected Poems of Wallace Stevens*. Copyright 1923, 1931, 1954 by Wallace Stevens; "A Rabbit as King of the Ghosts" from *The Collected Poems of Wallace Stevens*. Copyright 1942, 1954 by Wallace Stevens; "Escape" from *The Collected Poems of Elinor Wylie*. Copyright 1921, 1932 by Alfred A. Knopf, Inc. The Macmillan Company, "Snow in the Suburbs" from *Collected Poems* by Thomas Hardy; "Time, you old gipsy man" from *Poems* by Ralph Hodgson; "The Cat and the Moon," "The Happy Townland," "The Song of Wandering Aengus," "To a Squirrel at Kyle-na-no" from *Collected Poems* by W. B. Yeats. Mrs. Harold Monro, "Milk for the Cat" and "Overheard on a Saltmarsh" from *Collected Poems* by Harold Monro. New Directions, "The Gypsy" from *Personae* by Ezra Pound. Copyright 1926, 1952 by Ezra Pound, reprinted by permission of the publisher, New Directions; "Fern Hill" from *The Collected Poems of Dylan Thomas*. Copyright 1953 by Dylan Thomas, reprinted by permission of the publisher, New Directions; "Poem," "Spring and All," "The Term" from *The Collected Earlier Poems* by William Carlos Williams. Copyright 1951 by William Carlos Williams, reprinted by permission of the publisher, New Directions. Oxford University Press, Inc., "Pied Beauty," "Spring and Fall," "The Starlight Night" from *Poems* by Gerard Manley Hopkins. Mr. A. D. Peters, "Kilcash" by Frank O'Connor. Miss E. J. Scovell and the Cresset Press, Ltd., "The Boy Fishing" from *Shadows of Chrysanthemums* by E. J. Scovell. Sidgwick & Jackson, Ltd., "Romance" from *Collected Poems* by Walter James Turner. Mr. Andrew Young and Jonathan Cape, Ltd., "The Shepherd's Hut" and "A Windy Day" from *Collected Poems* by Andrew Young.

THIS WAY, DELIGHT

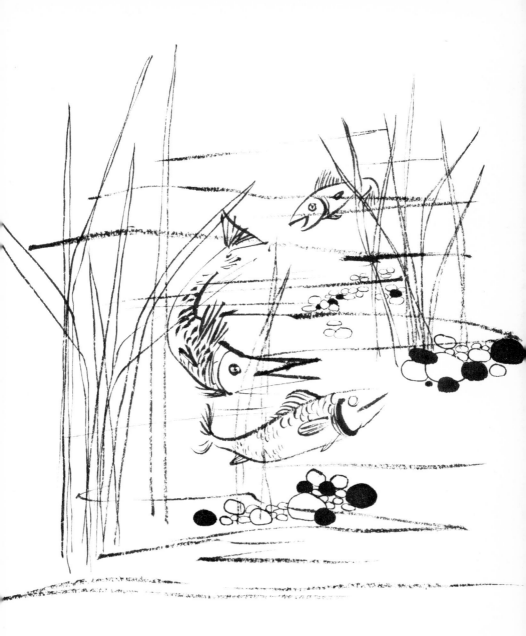

CHARMS

Explanation, on Coming Home Late

We went down to the river's brink
To of those clear waters drink,
Where the fishes, gold and red,
Ever quickly past us sped,

And the pebbles, red and blue,
Which we saw the green weeds through
At the bottom shining lay:
It was their shining made us stay.

RICHARD HUGHES (aged 7)

The Boy Fishing

I am cold and alone,
On my tree-root sitting as still as a stone.
The fish come to my net. I scorned the sun,
The voices on the road, and they have gone.
My eyes are buried in the cold pond, under
The cold, spread leaves; my thoughts are silver-wet.
I have ten stickleback, a half-day's plunder,
Safe in my jar. I shall have ten more yet.

E. J. SCOVELL

The Shepherd's Hut

Now when I could not find the road
Unless beside it also flowed
This cobbled beck that through the night,
Breaking on stones, makes its own light,
Where blackness in the starlit sky
Is all I know a mountain by,
A shepherd little thinks how far
His lamp is shining like a star.

ANDREW YOUNG

10

Four Ducks on a Pond

Four ducks on a pond,
A grass-bank beyond,
A blue sky of spring,
White clouds on the wing;
What a little thing
To remember for years—
To remember with tears!

WILLIAM ALLINGHAM

Spring and All

so much depends
upon

a red wheel
barrow

glazed with rain
water

beside the white
chickens

WILLIAM CARLOS WILLIAMS

In Glencullen

Thrush, linnet, stare and wren,
Brown lark beside the sun,
Take thought of kestril, sparrow-hawk,
Birdlime and roving gun.

You great-great-grand-children
Of birds I've listened to,
I think I robbed your ancestors
When I was young as you.

JOHN M. SYNGE

Ploughing on Sunday

The white cock's tail
Tosses in the wind.
The turkey-cock's tail
Glitters in the sun.

Water in the fields.
The wind pours down.
The feathers flare
And bluster in the wind.

Remus, blow your horn!
I'm ploughing on Sunday,
Ploughing North America.
Blow your horn!

Tum-ti-tum,
Ti-tum-tum-tum!
The turkey-cock's tail
Spreads to the sun.

The white cock's tail
Streams to the moon.
Water in the fields.
The wind pours down.

WALLACE STEVENS

Old Cat Care

Green-eyed Care
May prowl and glare
And poke his snub, be-whiskered nose:
But Door fits tight
Against the Night:
Through criss-cross cracks no evil goes.

Window is small:
No room at all
For Worry and Money, his shoulder-bones:
Chimney is wide,
But Smoke's inside
And happy Smoke would smother his moans.

Be-whiskered Care
May prowl out there:
But I never heard
He caught the Blue Bird.

RICHARD HUGHES

Milk for the Cat

When the tea is brought at five o'clock,
And all the neat curtains are drawn with care,
The little black cat with bright green eyes
Is suddenly purring there.

At first she pretends, having nothing to do,
She has come in merely to blink by the grate,
But, though tea may be late or the milk may be sour,
She is never late.

And presently her agate eyes
Take a soft large milky haze,
And her independent casual glance
Becomes a stiff, hard gaze.

Then she stamps her claws or lifts her ears,
Or twists her tail and begins to stir,
Till suddenly all her lithe body becomes
One breathing, trembling purr.

The children eat and wriggle and laugh;
The two old ladies stroke their silk:
But the cat is grown small and thin with desire,
Transformed to a creeping lust for milk.

The white saucer like some full moon descends
At last from the clouds of the table above;
She sighs and dreams and thrills and glows,
Transfigured with love.

She nestles over the shining rim,
Buries her chin in the creamy sea;
Her tail hangs loose; each drowsy paw
Is doubled under each bending knee.

A long, dim ecstasy holds her life;
Her world is an infinite shapeless white,
Till her tongue has curled the last holy drop,
Then she sinks back into the night,

Draws and dips her body to heap
Her sleepy nerves in the great arm-chair,
Lies defeated and buried deep
Three or four hours unconscious there.

HAROLD MONRO

The Cat and the Moon

The cat went here and there
And the moon spun round like a top,
And the nearest kin of the moon,
The creeping cat, looked up.
Black Minnaloushe stared at the moon,
For, wander and wail as he would,
The pure cold light in the sky
Troubled his animal blood.
Minnaloushe runs in the grass
Lifting his delicate feet.
Do you dance, Minnaloushe, do you dance?
When two close kindred meet,
What better than call a dance?
Maybe the moon may learn,
Tired of that courtly fashion,
A new dance turn.
Minnaloushe creeps through the grass
From moonlit place to place,
The sacred moon overhead
Has taken a new phase.
Does Minnaloushe know that his pupils
Will pass from change to change,
And that from round to crescent,
From crescent to round they range?
Minnaloushe creeps through the grass
Alone, important and wise,
And lifts to the changing moon
His changing eyes.

W. B. YEATS

Poem

As the cat
climbed over
the top of

the jamcloset
first the right
forefoot

carefully
then the hind
stepped down

into the pit of
the empty
flowerpot

WILLIAM CARLOS WILLIAMS

A Rabbit as King of the Ghosts

The difficulty to think at the end of the day,
When the shapeless shadow covers the sun
And nothing is left except light on your fur—

There was the cat slopping its milk all day,
Fat cat, red tongue, green mind, white milk
And August the most peaceful month.

To be, in the grass, in the peacefullest time,
Without that monument of cat,
The cat forgotten in the moon;

And to feel that the light is a rabbit-light,
In which everything is meant for you
And nothing need be explained;

Then there is nothing to think of. It comes of itself;
And east rushes west and west rushes down,
No matter. The grass is full

And full of yourself. The trees around are for you,
The whole of the wideness of night is for you,
A self that touches all edges,

You become a self that fills the four corners of night.
The red cat hides away in the fur-light
And there you are humped high, humped up,

You are humped higher and higher, black as stone—
You sit with your head like a carving in space
And the little green cat is a bug in the grass.

WALLACE STEVENS

Janet Waking

Beautifully Janet slept
Till it was deeply morning. She woke then
And thought about her dainty-feathered hen,
To see how it had kept.

One kiss she gave her mother,
Only a small one gave she her daddy
Who would have kissed each curl of his shining baby;
No kiss at all for her brother.

"Old Chucky, old Chucky!" she cried,
Running across the world upon the grass
To Chucky's house, and listening. But alas,
Her Chucky had died.

It was a transmogrifying bee
Came droning down on Chucky's old bald head
And sat and put the poison. It scarcely bled,
But how exceedingly

And purply did the knot
Swell with the venom and communicate
Its rigor! Now the poor comb stood up straight
But Chucky did not.

So there was Janet
Kneeling on the wet grass, crying her brown hen
(Translated far beyond the daughters of men)
To rise and walk upon it.

And weeping fast as she had breath
Janet implored us, "Wake her from her sleep!"
And would not be instructed in how deep
Was the forgetful kingdom of death.

JOHN CROWE RANSOM

Three Turkeys

Three turkeys fair their last have breathed
And now this world for ever leaved
Their Father & their Mother too
Will sigh and weep as well as you
Mourning for their osprings fair
Whom they did nurse with tender care
Indeed the rats their bones have cranched
To eternity they are launched
There graceful form and pretty eyes
Their fellow fows did not despise
A direful death indeed they had
That would put any parent mad
But she was more than unual calm
She did not give a single dam
She is as genteel as a lamb
Here ends this melancholy lay
Farewell Poor Turkeys I must say

MARJORIE FLEMING (aged 7)

A Dirge

Call for the robin-redbreast and the wren,
Since o'er shady groves they hover
And with leaves and flowers do cover
The friendless bodies of unburied men.
Call unto his funeral dole
The ant, the field-mouse, and the mole,
To rear him hillocks that shall keep him warm
And, when gay tombs are robbed, sustain no harm;
But keep the wolf far thence, that's foe to men,
For with his nails he'll dig them up again.

JOHN WEBSTER

Song — The Owl

I

When cats run home and light is come,
　And dew is cold upon the ground,
And the far-off stream is dumb,
　And the whirring sail goes round,
　And the whirring sail goes round;
　　Alone and warming his five wits,
　　The white owl in the belfry sits.

II

When merry milkmaids click the latch,
　And rarely smells the new-mown hay,
And the cock hath sung beneath the thatch
　Twice or thrice his roundelay,
　Twice or thrice his roundelay;
　　Alone and warming his five wits,
　　The white owl in the belfry sits.

ALFRED TENNYSON

Overheard on a Saltmarsh

Nymph, nymph, what are your beads?

Green glass, goblin. Why do you stare at them?

Give them me.

     No.

Give them me. Give them me.

          No.

Then I will howl all night in the reeds,
Lie in the mud and howl for them.

Goblin, why do you love them so?

They are better than stars or water,
Better than voices of winds that sing,
Better than any man's fair daughter,
Your green glass beads on a silver ring.

Hush, I stole them out of the moon.

Give me your beads, I want them.

          No.

I will howl in a deep lagoon
For your green glass beads, I love them so.
Give them me. Give them.

     No.

HAROLD MONRO

The Witches' Charms

1 *Charm.* Dame, dame! the watch is set:
Quickly come, we all are met.
From the lakes and from the fens,
From the rocks and from the dens,
From the woods and from the caves,
From the churchyards, from the graves,
From the dungeon, from the tree
That they die on, here are we!

> Comes she not yet?
> Strike another heat!

2 *Charm.* The weather is fair, the wind is good:
Up, dame, o' your horse of wood!
Or else tuck up your gray frock,
And saddle your goat or your green cock,
And make his bridle a bottom of thrid
To roll up how many miles you have rid.
Quickly come away,
For we all stay.

> Not yet? nay then
> We'll try her again.

3 *Charm.* The owl is abroad, the bat and the toad,
    And so is the cat-a-mountain;
The ant and the mole sit both in a hole,
    And frog peeps out o' the fountain.
The dogs they do bay, and the timbrels play,
    The spindle is now a-turning;
The moon it is red, and the stars are fled,
    But all the sky is a-burning:
The ditch is made, and our nails the spade:
With pictures full, of wax and of wool,
Their livers I stick with needles quick;
There lacks but the blood to make up the flood.
Quickly, dame, then bring your part in!
Spur, spur, upon little Martin!
Merrily, merrily, make him sail,
A worm in his mouth and a thorn in 's tail,
Fire above, and fire below,
With a whip i' your hand to make him go!

        O now she's come!
        Let all be dumb.

                    BEN JONSON

The Song of Wandering Aengus

I went out to the hazel wood,
Because a fire was in my head,
And cut and peeled a hazel wand,
And hooked a berry to a thread;
And when white moths were on the wing,
And moth-like stars were flickering out,
I dropped the berry in a stream,
And caught a little silver trout.

When I had laid it on the floor
I went to blow the fire aflame,
But something rustled on the floor,
And someone called me by my name;
It had become a glimmering girl
With apple blossom in her hair
Who called me by my name and ran
And faded through the brightening air.

Though I am old with wandering
Through hollow lands and hilly lands,
I will find out where she has gone,
And kiss her lips and take her hands;
And walk among long dappled grass,
And pluck till time and times are done
The silver apples of the moon,
The golden apples of the sun.

W. B. YEATS

Puck Speaks

Now the hungry lion roars,
  And the wolf behowls the moon;
Whilst the heavy ploughman snores,
  All with weary task fordone.
Now the wasted brands do glow,
  Whilst the screech-owl, screeching loud,
Puts the wretch that lies in woe
  In remembrance of a shroud.
Now it is the time of night
  That the graves, all gaping wide,
Every one lets forth his sprite,
  In the church-way paths to glide;
And we fairies, that do run
  By the triple Hecate's team,
From the presence of the sun,
  Following darkness like a dream,
Now we frolic: not a mouse
Shall disturb this hallow'd house:
I am sent with broom before,
To sweep the dust behind the door.

WILLIAM SHAKESPEARE

Song

I had a dove and the sweet dove died;
   And I have thought it died of grieving:
O, what could it grieve for? it was tied,
   With a silken thread of my own hand's weaving;
Sweet little red feet! why did you die—
Why would you leave me, sweet dove! why?
You liv'd alone on the forest-tree,
Why, pretty thing! could you not live with me?
I kiss'd you oft and gave you white peas;
Why not live sweetly, as in the green trees?

JOHN KEATS

Answer to a Child's Question

Do you ask what the birds say? The Sparrow, the Dove,
The Linnet and Thrush say, "I love and I love!"
In the winter they're silent—the wind is so strong;
What it says, I don't know, but it sings a loud song.
But green leaves, and blossoms, and sunny warm weather,
And singing, and loving—all come back together.
But the Lark is so brimful of gladness and love,
The green fields below him, the blue sky above,
That he sings, and he sings; and for ever sings he—
"I love my Love, and my Love loves me!"

SAMUEL TAYLOR COLERIDGE

This is the Key

This is the Key of the Kingdom:
In that Kingdom is a city;
In that city is a town;
In that town there is a street;
In that street there winds a lane;
In that lane there is a yard;
In that yard there is a house;
In that house there waits a room;
In that room an empty bed;
And on that bed a basket—
A Basket of Sweet Flowers:
    Of Flowers, of Flowers;
    A basket of Sweet Flowers.

Flowers in a basket;
Basket on the bed;
Bed in the chamber;
Chamber in the house;
House in the weedy yard;
Yard in the winding lane;
Lane in the broad street;
Street in the high town;
Town in the city;
City in the Kingdom—
This is the Key of the Kingdom.
    Of the Kingdom this is the Key.

UNKNOWN

Lady will you come with me into

Lady will you come with me into
the extremely little house of
my mind. Clocks strike. The

moon's round, through the window

as you see and really i have no
servants. We could almost live

at the top of these stairs, there's a free
room. We almost could go (you
and i) into a together whitely big
there is but if so or so

slowly i opened the window a
most tinyness, the moon (with white wig
and polished buttons) would take you away

—and all the clocks would run down the next day.

E. E. CUMMINGS

To a Squirrel at Kyle-na-no

Come play with me;
Why should you run
Through the shaking tree
As though I'd a gun
To strike you dead?
When all I would do
Is to scratch your head
And let you go.

W. B. YEATS

Earthy Anecdote

Every time the bucks went clattering
Over Oklahoma
A firecat bristled in the way.

Wherever they went,
They went clattering,
Until they swerved
In a swift, circular line
To the right,
Because of the firecat.

Or until they swerved
In a swift, circular line
To the left,
Because of the firecat.

The bucks clattered.
The firecat went leaping,
To the right, to the left,
And
Bristled in the way.

Later, the firecat closed his bright eyes
And slept.

WALLACE STEVENS

Poem

I'll tell you how the sun rose,—
A ribbon at a time.
The steeples swam in amethyst,
The news like squirrels ran.

The hills untied their bonnets,
The bobolinks begun.
Then I said softly to myself,
"That must have been the sun!"

. . . . .

But how he set, I know not.
There seemed a purple stile
Which little yellow boys and girls
Were climbing all the while

Till when they reached the other side,
A dominie in gray
Put gently up the evening bars,
And led the flock away.

EMILY DICKINSON

SONGS

Introduction

Piping down the valleys wild,
Piping songs of pleasant glee,
On a cloud I saw a child,
And he laughing said to me:

"Pipe a song about a Lamb!"
So I piped with merry chear.
"Piper, pipe that song again;"
So I piped: he wept to hear.

"Drop thy pipe, thy happy pipe;
"Sing thy songs of happy chear:"
So I sung the same again,
While he wept with joy to hear.

"Piper, sit thee down and write
"In a book, that all may read."
So he vanish'd from my sight,
And I pluck'd a hollow reed,

And I made a rural pen,
And I stain'd the water clear,
And I wrote my happy songs
Every child may joy to hear.

WILLIAM BLAKE

Infant Joy

"I have no name:
"I am but two days old."
What shall I call thee?
"I happy am,
"Joy is my name."
Sweet joy befall thee!

Pretty joy!
Sweet joy but two days old,
Sweet joy I call thee:
Thou dost smile,
I sing the while,
Sweet joy befall thee!

WILLIAM BLAKE

The Blossom

Merry, Merry Sparrow!
Under leaves so green
A happy Blossom
Sees you swift as arrow
Seek your cradle narrow
Near my Bosom.

Pretty, Pretty Robin!
Under leaves so green
A happy Blossom
Hears you sobbing, sobbing,
Pretty, Pretty Robin,
Near my Bosom.

WILLIAM BLAKE

The Shepherd

How sweet is the Shepherd's sweet lot!
From the morn to the evening he strays;
He shall follow his sheep all the day,
And his tongue shall be filled with praise.

For he hears the lamb's innocent call,
And he hears the ewe's tender reply;
He is watchful while they are in peace,
For they know when their Shepherd is nigh.

WILLIAM BLAKE

40

The Passionate Shepherd to his Love

Come live with me and be my love,
And we will all the pleasures prove,
That hills and valleys, dales and fields,
And all the craggy mountains yields.

There we will sit upon the rocks,
And see the shepherds feed their flocks,
By shallow rivers to whose falls
Melodious birds sing madrigals.

And I will make thee beds of roses
With a thousand fragrant posies,
A cap of flowers, and a kirtle
Embroidered all with leaves of myrtle;

A gown made of the finest wool
Which from our pretty lambs we pull;
Fair lined slippers for the cold,
With buckles of the purest gold;

A belt of straw and ivy buds,
With coral clasps and amber studs:
And if these pleasures may thee move,
Come live with me and be my love.

The shepherds' swains shall dance and sing
For thy delight each May morning:
If these delights thy mind may move,
Then live with me and be my love.

CHRISTOPHER MARLOWE

41

Daphnis to Ganymede

If thou wilt come and dwell with me at home,
My sheep-cote shall be strowed with new green rushes;
We'll haunt the trembling prickets as they roam
About the fields, along the hawthorn bushes:
   I have a piebald cur to hunt the hare:
   So we will live with dainty forest fare.

Nay, more than this, I have a garden plot,
Wherein there wants nor herbs, nor roots, nor flowers,—
Flowers to smell, roots to eat, herbs for the pot,—
And dainty shelters when the welkin lours:
   Sweet smelling beds of lilies and of roses,
   Which rosemary banks and lavender encloses.

There grows the gillyflower, the mint, the daisy
Both red and white, the blue-veined violet,
The purple hyacinth, the spike to please thee,
The scarlet-dyed carnation bleeding yet,
   The sage, the savory, the sweet marjoram,
   Hyssop, thyme, and eye-bright, good for the blind and dumb;

The pink, the primrose, cowslip, and daffadilly,
The harebell blue, the crimson columbine,
Sage, lettuce, parsley, and the milk-white lily,
The rose, and speckled flower called sops-in-wine,
   Fine pretty kingcups, and the yellow boots
   That grows by rivers, and by shallow brooks;

And many thousand moe, I cannot name,
Of herbs and flowers that in gardens grow,
I have for thee; and conies that be tame,
Young rabbits, white as swan, and black as crow,
   Some speckled here and there with dainty spots;
   And more, I have two milch and milk-white goats.

And these, and more, I'll give thee for thy love,
If these, and more, may tice thy love away:
I have a pigeon-house, in it a dove,
Which I love more than mortal tongue can say;
  And, last of all, I'll give thee a little lamb
    To play withal, new weanëd from her dam.

RICHARD BARNFIELD

Song

The maidens came
  When I was in my mother's bower;
I had all that I would.
    The bailey beareth the bell away;
    The lily, the rose, the rose I lay.
The silver is white, red is the gold;
The robes they lay in fold.
    The bailey beareth the bell away;
    The lily, the rose, the rose I lay.
And through the glass window shines the sun.
How should I love, and I so young?
    The bailey beareth the bell away;
    The lily, the lily, the rose I lay.

UNKNOWN

Song

Do not fear to put thy feet
Naked in the river sweet;
Think not leech, or newt, or toad,
Will bite thy foot, when thou hast trod:
Nor let the water rising high,
As thou wad'st in, make thee cry
And sob; but ever live with me,
And not a wave shall trouble thee!

JOHN FLETCHER

Song

The feathers of the willow
Are half of them grown yellow
   Above the swelling stream;
And ragged are the bushes,
And rusty now the rushes,
   And wild the clouded gleam.

The thistle now is older,
His stalk begins to moulder,
   His head is white as snow;
The branches all are barer,
The linnet's song is rarer,
   The robin pipeth now.

RICHARD WATSON DIXON

A Birthday

My heart is like a singing bird
   Whose nest is in a watered shoot:
My heart is like an apple-tree
   Whose boughs are bent with thickset fruit;
My heart is like a rainbow shell
   That paddles in a halcyon sea;
My heart is gladder than all these
   Because my love is come to me.

Raise me a dais of silk and down;
   Hang it with vair and purple dyes;
Carve it in doves and pomegranates,
   And peacocks with a hundred eyes;
Work it in gold and silver grapes,
   In leaves and silver fleurs-de-lys;
Because the birthday of my life
   Is come, my love is come to me.

CHRISTINA ROSSETTI

Song

And can the physician make sick men well?
And can the magician a fortune divine?
Without lily, germander, and sops-in-wine?
> With sweet-briar
> And bon-fire
> And strawberry wire
> And columbine.

Within and without, in and out, round as a ball,
With hither and thither, as straight as a line,
With lily, germander, and sops-in-wine,
> With sweet-briar
> And bon-fire
> And strawberry wire
> And columbine.

When Saturn did live, there lived no poor,
The king and the beggar with roots did dine,
With lily, germander, and sops-in-wine,
> With sweet-briar
> And bon-fire
> And strawberry wire
> And columbine.

UNKNOWN

The Basket-Maker's Song

Art thou poor, yet hast thou golden slumbers?
    O sweet content!
Art thou rich, yet is thy mind perplexed?
    O punishment!
Dost thou laugh to see how fools are vexed
To add to golden numbers, golden numbers?
O sweet content! O sweet content!
    Work apace, apace, apace, apace;
    Honest labour bears a lovely face;
    Then hey nonny nonny, hey nonny nonny!

Canst drink the waters of the crisped spring?
    O sweet content!
Swim'st thou in wealth, yet sink'st in thine own tears?
    O punishment!
Then he that patiently want's burden bears
No burden bears, but is a king, a king!
O sweet content! O sweet content!
    Work apace, apace, apace, apace;
    Honest labour bears a lovely face;
    Then hey nonny nonny, hey nonny nonny!

THOMAS DEKKER

Art thou gone in haste?

Art thou gone in haste?
  I'll not forsake thee!
Runn'st thou ne'er so fast,
  I'll o'ertake thee!
O'er the dales or the downs,
  Through the green meadows,
From the fields, through the towns,
  To the dim shadows!

All along the plain,
  To the low fountains;
Up and down again,
  From the high mountains:
Echo, then, shall again
  Tell her I follow,
And the floods to the woods
  Carry my holla.
          Holla!
Ce! la! ho! ho! hu!

UNKNOWN

Celanta at the Well of Life

Gently dip, but not too deep,
For fear you make the golden beard to weep.
Fair maiden, white and red,
Comb me smooth, and stroke my head,
And thou shalt have some cockell-bread.
Gently dip, but not too deep,
For fear thou make the golden beard to weep.
Fair maid, white and red,
Comb me smooth, and stroke my head,
And every hair a sheaf shall be,
And every sheaf a golden tree.

GEORGE PEELE

Song

O'er the smooth enamel'd green
Where no print of step hath been,
      Follow me as I sing,
      And touch the warbled string.
Under the shady roof
Of branching Elm-Star-proof.
      Follow me,
I will bring you where she sits
Clad in splendor as befits
      Her deity.
Such a rural Queen
All *Arcadia* hath not seen.

JOHN MILTON

Pack, clouds, away

Pack, clouds, away, and welcome day,
   With night we banish sorrow;
Sweet air, blow soft; mount, lark, aloft
     To give my Love good-morrow!
Wings from the wind, to please her mind,
   Notes from the lark I'll borrow;
Bird, prune thy wing, nightingale, sing,
    To give my Love good-morrow!
     To give my Love good-morrow
     Notes from them all I'll borrow,

Wake from the nest, robin-redbreast,
   Sing, birds, in every furrow;
And from each bill, let music shrill
    Give my fair Love good-morrow!
Blackbird and thrush in every bush,
   Stare, linnet, and cock-sparrow,
You pretty elves, amongst yourselves
    Sing my fair Love good-morrow!
     To give my Love good-morrow
     Sing, birds, in every furrow!

THOMAS HEYWOOD

In Just-spring

in Just-
spring   when the world is mud-
luscious the little
lame balloonman

whistles   far   and wee

and eddieandbill come
running from marbles and
piracies and it's
spring

when the world is puddle-wonderful

the queer
old balloonman whistles
far   and   wee
and bettyandisbel come dancing

from hop-scotch and jump-rope and

it's
spring
and
       the

              goat-footed

balloonman   whistles
far
and
wee

E. E. CUMMINGS

What bird so sings

What bird so sings, yet so does wail?
Oh, 'tis the ravished nightingale.
Jug, jug, jug, jug, tereu! she cries,
And still her woes at midnight rise.
Brave prick-song! who is't now we hear?
None but the lark so shrill and clear;
How at heaven's gates she claps her wings!--
The morn not waking till she sings.
Hark, hark, with what a pretty throat
Poor robin redbreast tunes his note!
Hark how the jolly cuckoos sing
Cuckoo! to welcome in the spring!
Cuckoo! to welcome in the spring!

JOHN LYLY (?)

Song in the Wood

This way, this way, come and hear,
You that hold these pleasures dear;
Fill your ears with our sweet sound,
Whilst we melt the frozen ground.
This way come; make haste, O fair!
Let your clear eyes gild the air;
Come, and bless us with your sight;
This way, this way, seek delight!

JOHN FLETCHER

Spring and Winter

When daisies pied and violets blue
   And lady-smocks all silver-white
And cuckoo-buds of yellow hue
   Do paint the meadows with delight,
The cuckoo then, on every tree,
Mocks married men; for thus sings he,
              Cuckoo;
Cuckoo, cuckoo: O word of fear,
Unpleasing to a married ear!

When shepherds pipe on oaten straws
   And merry larks are ploughmen's clocks,
When turtles tread, and rooks, and daws,
   And maidens bleach their summer smocks,
The cuckoo then, on every tree,
Mocks married men; for thus sings he,
              Cuckoo;
Cuckoo, cuckoo: O word of fear,
Unpleasing to a married ear!

When icicles hang by the wall
   And Dick the shepherd blows his nail
And Tom bears logs into the hall
   And milk comes frozen home in pail,
When blood is nipp'd and ways be foul,
Then nightly sings the staring owl,
              Tu-whit tu-who;
A merry note,
While greasy Joan doth keel the pot.

When all aloud the wind doth blow
    And coughing drowns the parson's saw
And birds sit brooding in the snow
    And Marian's nose looks red and raw,
When roasted crabs hiss in the bowl,
Then nightly sings the staring owl,
                    Tu-whit tu-who;
A merry note,
While greasy Joan doth keel the pot.

WILLIAM SHAKESPEARE

Ariel's Song

Come unto these yellow sands,
    And then take hands:
Curtsied when you have, and kiss'd—
    The wild waves whist;
Foot it featly here and there;
And, sweet sprites, the burthen bear.
     Hark, hark!
              Bow-wow.
     The watch-dogs bark:
              Bow-wow.
     Hark, hark! I hear
     The strain of strutting chanticleer
     Cry, Cock-a-diddle-dow.

WILLIAM SHAKESPEARE

Over hill, over dale

Over hill, over dale,
    Thorough bush, thorough brier,
Over park, over pale,
    Thorough flood, thorough fire,
I do wander every where,
Swifter than the moonès sphere;
And I serve the fairy queen,
To dew her orbs upon the green.
The cowslips tall her pensioners be:
In their gold coats spots you see;
Those be rubies, fairy favours,
In those freckles live their savours:
I must go seek some dewdrops here
And hang a pearl in every cowslip's ear.

WILLIAM SHAKESPEARE

Where the bee sucks

Where the bee sucks, there suck I:
In a cowslip's bell I lie;
There I couch when owls do cry.
On the bat's back I do fly
After summer merrily.
Merrily, merrily shall I live now
Under the blossom that hangs on the bough.

WILLIAM SHAKESPEARE

Immalee

I gather thyme upon the sunny hills,
    And its pure fragrance ever gladdens me,
    And in my mind having tranquillity
I smile to see how my green basket fills.
And by clear streams I gather daffodils;
    And in dim woods find out the cherry-tree,
    And take its fruit and the wild strawberry
And nuts and honey; and live free from ills.
I dwell on the green earth, 'neath the blue sky,
    Birds are my friends, and leaves my rustling roof:
The deer are not afraid of me, and I
    Hear the wild goat, and hail its hastening hoof;
The squirrels sit perked as I pass them by,
    And even the watchful hare stands not aloof.

CHRISTINA ROSSETTI

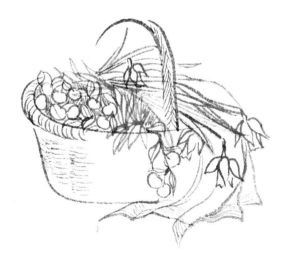

Spring and Fall:

TO A YOUNG CHILD

Márgarét, are you gríeving
Over Goldengrove unleaving?
Leáves, líke the things of man, you
With your fresh thoughts care for, can you?
Áh! ás the heart grows older
It will come to such sights colder
By and by, nor spare a sigh
Though worlds of wanwood leafmeal lie;
And yet you wíll weep and know why.
Now no matter, child, the name:
Sórrow's springs áre the same.
Nor mouth had, no nor mind, expressed
What heart heard of, ghost guessed:
It ís the blight man was born for,
It is Margaret you mourn for.

GERARD MANLEY HOPKINS

New Prince, New Pomp

Behold, a silly tender Babe
    In freezing winter night
In homely manger trembling lies,
    Alas, a piteous sight!

The inns are full; no man will yield
    This little pilgrim bed,
But forced he is with silly beasts
    In crib to shroud his head.

Despise him not for lying there,
    First, what he is inquire;
An orient pearl is often found
    In depth of dirty mire.

Weigh not his crib, his wooden dish,
    Nor beasts that by him feed;
Weigh not his Mother's poor attire,
    Nor Joseph's simple weed.

This stable is a Prince's court,
    This crib his chair of state;
The beasts are parcel of his pomp,
    The wooden dish his plate.

The persons in that poor attire
    His royal liveries wear;
The Prince himself is come from heaven;
    This pomp is prized there.

With joy approach, O Christian wight,
    Do homage to thy King;
And highly praise his humble pomp,
    Which he from heaven doth bring.

ROBERT SOUTHWELL

A New Year Carol

Here we bring new water
    from the well so clear,
For to worship God with,
    this happy New Year.

Sing levy dew, sing levy dew,
    the water and the wine;
The seven bright gold wires
    and the bugles that do shine.

Sing reign of Fair Maid,
    with gold upon her toe,—
Open you the West Door,
    and turn the Old Year go.

Sing reign of Fair Maid
    with gold upon her chin,—
Open you the East Door,
    and let the New Year in.

Sing levy dew, sing levy dew,
    the water and the wine;
The seven bright gold wires
    and the bugles they do shine.

UNKNOWN

Carol

I sing of a maiden
  That is makeless,
King of all kings
  To her son she ches,
He came all so still
  There his mother was,
As dew in April
  That falleth on the grass.
He came all so still
  To his mother's bower,
As dew in April
  That falleth on the flower.
He came all so still
  There his mother lay,
As dew in April
  That falleth on the spray.
Mother and maiden
  Was never none but she;
Well may such a lady
  God's mother be.

UNKNOWN

makeless—without a mate
ches—chose

To Mistress Margaret Hussey

Merry Margaret,
As midsummer flower,
Gentle as falcon
Or hawk of the tower;
   With solace and gladness,
Much mirth and no madness,
All good and no badness,
So joyously,
So maidenly,
So womanly
Her demeaning
In every thing,
Far, far passing
That I can endite,
Or suffice to write
Of merry Margaret,
As midsummer flower,
Gentle as falcon
Or hawk of the tower;
   As patient and as still,
And as full of good will,
As fair Ysaphill;
Coliaunder,
Sweet pomaunder,
Good Cassaunder;
Steadfast of thought,
Well made, well wrought;
Far may be sought

coliaunder—coriander
pomaunder—perfume-box
erst—before

Erst that ye can find
So courteous, so kind
As merry Margaret,
This midsummer flower,
Gentle as falcon
Or hawk of the tower.

JOHN SKELTON

There is a garden in her face

There is a garden in her face
   Where roses and white lilies grow;
A heavenly paradise is that place
   Wherein all pleasant fruits do flow.
There cherries grow which none may buy,
Till 'cherry-ripe' themselves do cry.

Those cherries fairly do enclose
   Of orient pearl a double row,
Which when her lovely laughter shows,
   They look like rosebuds filled with snow.
Yet them no peer nor prince can buy,
Till 'cherry-ripe' themselves do cry.

Her eyes like angels watch them still,
   Her brows like bended bows do stand,
Threatening with piercing frowns to kill
   All that attempt, with eye or hand,
Those sacred cherries to come nigh,
Till 'cherry-ripe' themselves do cry.

THOMAS CAMPION

To Morfydd

A voice on the winds,
A voice by the waters,
   Wanders and cries:
Oh! what are the winds?
And what are the waters?
   Mine are your eyes!

Western the winds are,
And western the waters,
   Where the light lies:
Oh! what are the winds?
And what are the waters?
   Mine are your eyes!

Cold, cold, grow the winds,
And wild grow the waters,
   Where the sun dies:
Oh! what are the winds?
And what are the waters?
   Mine are your eyes!

And down the night winds,
And down the night waters,
   The music flies:
Oh! what are the winds?
And what are the waters?
Cold be the winds,
And wild be the waters,
   So mine be your eyes!

LIONEL JOHNSON

A Song

A widow bird sate mourning for her love
    Upon a wintry bough;
The frozen wind crept on above,
    The freezing stream below.

There was no leaf upon the forest bare,
    No flower upon the ground,
And little motion in the air
    Except the mill-wheel's sound.

PERCY BYSSHE SHELLEY

Ariel's Dirge

Full fathom five thy father lies;
   Of his bones are coral made;
Those are pearls that were his eyes;
Nothing of him that doth fade
But doth suffer a sea-change
Into something rich and strange.
Sea-nymphs hourly ring his knell:
                  Ding-dong.
Hark! now I hear them,—Ding-dong, bell.

WILLIAM SHAKESPEARE

Song

Weep, weep, ye woodmen! wail;
   Your hands with sorrow wring!
Your master Robin Hood lies dead,
   Therefore sigh as you sing.

Here lies his primer and his beads,
   His bent bow and his arrows keen,
His good sword and his holy cross.
   Now cast on flowers fresh and green;

And, as they fall, shed tears and say
   Well-a, Well-a-day! well-a, well-a-day!
Thus cast ye flowers, and sing,
   And on to Wakefield take your way.

ANTHONY MUNDAY (?)

Song

The splendour falls on castle walls
    And snowy summits old in story:
The long light shakes across the lakes,
    And the wild cataract leaps in glory.
Blow, bugle, blow, set the wild echoes flying,
Blow, bugle; answer, echoes, dying, dying, dying.

O hark, O hear! how thin and clear,
    And thinner, clearer, farther going!
O sweet and far from cliff and scar
    The horns of Elfland faintly blowing!
Blow, let us hear the purple glens replying:
Blow, bugle; answer, echoes, dying, dying, dying.

O love, they die in yon rich sky,
    They faint on hill or field or river:
Our echoes roll from soul to soul,
    And grow for ever and for ever.
Blow, bugle, blow, set the wild echoes flying,
And answer, echoes, answer, dying, dying, dying.

ALFRED TENNYSON

72

Song

Sweet and low, sweet and low,
   Wind of the western sea,
Low, low, breathe and blow,
   Wind of the western sea!
Over the rolling waters go,
Come from the dying moon, and blow,
   Blow him again to me;
While my little one, while my pretty one, sleeps.

Sleep and rest, sleep and rest,
   Father will come to thee soon;
Rest, rest, on mother's breast,
   Father will come to thee soon;
Father will come to his babe in the nest,
Silver sails all out of the west
   Under the silver moon:
Sleep, my little one, sleep, my pretty one, sleep.

ALFRED TENNYSON

Nurse's Song

(FROM THE GERMAN)

Sleep, baby, sleep!
Your father herds his sheep:
Your mother shakes the little tree
From which fall pretty dreams on thee;
      Sleep, baby, sleep!

Sleep, baby, sleep!
The heavens are white with sheep;
For they are lambs—those stars so bright:
And the moon's the shepherd of the night;
      Sleep, baby, sleep!

Sleep, baby, sleep!
And I'll give thee a sheep,
Which, with its golden bell, shall be
A little play-fellow for thee;
      Sleep, baby, sleep!

Sleep, baby, sleep!
And bleat not like a sheep,
Or else the shepherd's angry dog
Will come and bite my naughty rogue;
      Sleep, baby, sleep!

Sleep, baby, sleep!
Go out and herd the sheep,
Go out, you barking black dog, go,
And waken not my baby so;
      Sleep, baby, sleep!

UNKNOWN

Nurse's Song

When the voices of children are heard on the green
And laughing is heard on the hill,
My heart is at rest within my breast
    And everything else is still.

"Then come home, my children, the sun is gone down
"And the dews of night arise;
"Come, come, leave off play, and let us away
"Till the morning appears in the skies."

"No, no, let us play, for it is yet day
"And we cannot go to sleep;
"Besides, in the skies the little birds fly
"And the hills are all cover'd with sheep."

"Well, well, go and play till the light fades away
"And then go home to bed."
The little ones leaped and shouted and laugh'd
    And all the hills echoed.

WILLIAM BLAKE

Laughing Song

When the green woods laugh with the voice of joy,
And the dimpling stream runs laughing by;
When the air does laugh with our merry wit,
And the green hill laughs with the noise of it;

When the meadows laugh with lively green,
And the grasshopper laughs in the merry scene,
When Mary and Susan and Emily
With their sweet round mouths sing "Ha, Ha, He!"

When the painted birds laugh in the shade,
When our table with cherries and nuts is spread,
Come live and be merry, and join with me,
To sing the sweet chorus of "Ha, Ha, He!"

WILLIAM BLAKE

Hunting Song

Up, up! ye dames, and lasses gay!
To the meadows trip away.
'Tis you must tend the flocks this morn,
And scare the small birds from the corn.
   Not a soul at home may stay:
     For the shepherds must go
     With lance and bow
   To hunt the wolf in the woods to-day.

Leave the hearth and leave the house
To the cricket and the mouse:
Find grannam out a sunny seat,
With babe and lambkin at her feet.
   Not a soul at home may stay:
     For the shepherds must go
     With lance and bow
   To hunt the wolf in the woods to-day.

SAMUEL TAYLOR COLERIDGE

Song

I have twelve oxen that be fair and brown,
And they go a-grazing down by the town.
    With hey! with how! with hey!
Sawest you not mine oxen, you little pretty boy?

I have twelve oxen, and they be fair and white,
And they go a-grazing down by the dyke.
    With hey! with how! with hey!
Sawest not you mine oxen, you little pretty boy?

I have twelve oxen, and they be fair and black,
And they go a-grazing down by the lake.
    With hey! with how! with hey!
Sawest not you mine oxen, you little pretty boy?

I have twelve oxen, and they be fair and red,
And they go a-grazing down by the mead.
    With hey! with how! with hey!
Sawest not you mine oxen, you little pretty boy?

UNKNOWN

Grace for a Child

Here a little child I stand
Heaving up my either hand;
Cold as paddocks though they be,
Here I lift them up to Thee,
For a benison to fall
On our meat, and on us all. *Amen.*

ROBERT HERRICK

paddocks—frogs

Song

Christ keep the Hollow Land
   Through the sweet springtide,
When the apple-blossoms bless
   The lowly bent hill side.

Christ keep the Hollow Land
   All the summer-tide;
Still we cannot understand
   Where the waters glide:

Only dimly seeing them
   Coldly slipping through
Many green-lipped cavern mouths
   Where the hills are blue.

WILLIAM MORRIS

ENCHANTMENTS

Written in March

*while resting on the Bridge at the Foot of
Brother's Water*

The cock is crowing,
The stream is flowing,
The small birds twitter,
The lake doth glitter,
The green field sleeps in the sun;
The oldest and youngest
Are at work with the strongest;
The cattle are grazing,
Their heads never raising;
There are forty feeding like one!

Like an army defeated
The snow hath retreated,
And now doth fare ill
On the top of the bare hill;
The ploughboy is whooping—anon—anon:
There's joy in the mountains;
There's life in the fountains;
Small clouds are sailing,
Blue sky prevailing;
The rain is over and gone!

WILLIAM WORDSWORTH

Cape Ann

O quick quick quick, quick hear the song-sparrow,
Swamp-sparrow, fox-sparrow, vesper-sparrow
At dawn and dusk. Follow the dance
Of the goldfinch at noon. Leave to chance
The Blackburnian warbler, the shy one. Hail
With shrill whistle the note of the quail, the bob-white
Dodging by bay-bush. Follow the feet
Of the walker, the water-thrush. Follow the flight
Of the dancing arrow, the purple martin. Greet
In silence the bullbat. All are delectable. Sweet sweet sweet
But resign this land at the end, resign it
To its true owner, the tough one, the sea-gull.
The palaver is finished.

T. S. ELIOT

The Starlight Night

Look at the stars! look, look up at the skies!
  O look at all the fire-folk sitting in the air!
  The bright boroughs, the circle-citadels there!
Down in dim woods the diamond delves! the elves'-eyes!
The grey lawns cold where gold, where quickgold lies!
  Wind-beat whitebeam! airy abeles set on a flare!
  Flake-doves sent floating forth at a farmyard scare!—
Ah well! it is all a purchase, all is a prize.

Buy then! bid then!—What?—Prayer, patience, alms, vows.
Look, look: a May-ness, like on orchard boughs!
  Look! March-bloom, like on mealed-with-yellow sallows!
These are indeed the barn; withindoors house
The shocks. This piece-bright paling shuts the spouse
  Christ home, Christ and his mother and all his hallows.

GERARD MANLEY HOPKINS

All That's Past

Very old are the woods;
   And the buds that break
Out of the brier's boughs,
   When March winds wake,
So old with their beauty are—
   Oh, no man knows
Through what wild centuries
   Roves back the rose.

Very old are the brooks;
   And the rills that rise
Where snow sleeps cold beneath
   The azure skies
Sing such a history
   Of come and gone,
Their every drop is as wise
   As Solomon.

Very old are we men;
   Our dreams are tales
Told in dim Eden
   By Eve's nightingales;
We wake and whisper awhile,
   But, the day gone by,
Silence and sleep like fields
   Of amaranth lie.

WALTER DE LA MARE

Kilcash

What shall we do for timber?
The last of the woods is down,
Kilcash and the house of its glory
And the bell of the house are gone;
The spot where her lady waited
That shamed all women for grace
When earls came sailing to greet her
And Mass was said in that place.

My cross and my affliction
Your gates are taken away,
Your avenue needs attention,
Goats in the garden stray;
Your courtyard's filled with water
And the great earls where are they?
The earls, the lady, the people
Beaten into the clay.

No sound of duck or of geese there
Hawk's cry or eagle's call,
Nor humming of the bees there
That brought honey and wax for all,
Nor the sweet gentle song of the birds there
When the sun has gone down to the West
Nor a cuckoo atop of the boughs there
Singing the world to rest.

There's a mist there tumbling from branches
Unstirred by night and by day,
And a darkness falling from heaven,
And our fortunes have ebbed away;
There's no holly nor hazel nor ash there
But pastures of rock and stone,
The crown of the forest is withered
And the last of its game is gone.

I beseech of Mary and Jesus
That the great come home again
With long dances danced in the garden
Fiddle music and mirth among men,
That Kilcash the home of our fathers
Be lifted on high again
And from that to the deluge of waters
In bounty and peace remain.

FRANK O'CONNOR

The Deserted House

There's no smoke in the chimney,
   And the rain beats on the floor;
There's no glass in the window,
   There's no wood in the door;
The heather grows behind the house,
   And the sand lies before.

No hand hath trained the ivy,
   The walls are gray and bare;
The boats upon the sea sail by,
   Nor ever tarry there.
No beast of the field comes nigh,
   Nor any bird of the air.

MARY COLERIDGE

Pied Beauty

Glory be to God for dappled things—
    For skies of couple-colour as a brinded cow;
      For rose-moles all in stipple upon trout that swim;
Fresh-firecoal chestnut falls; finches' wings;
    Landscape plotted and pieced—fold, fallow and plough;
      And áll trádes, their gear and tackle and trim.

All things counter, original, spare, strange;
    Whatever is fickle, freckled (who knows how?)
      With swift, slow; sweet, sour; adazzle, dim;
He fathers-forth whose beauty is past change:
              Praise him.

GERARD MANLEY HOPKINS

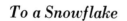

To a Snowflake

What heart could have thought you?—
Past our devisal
(O filigree petal!)
Fashioned so purely,
Fragilely, surely,
From what Paradisal
Imagineless metal,
Too costly for cost?
Who hammered you, wrought you,
From argentine vapour?—
'God was my shaper.
Passing surmisal,
He hammered, He wrought me,
From curled silver vapour,
To lust of His mind:—
Thou could'st not have thought me!
So purely, so palely,
Tinily, surely,
Mightily, frailly,
Insculped and embossed,
With His hammer of wind,
And His graver of frost.

FRANCIS THOMPSON

To Jane: the Invitation

Radiant Sister of the Day,
Awake! arise! and come away!
To the wild woods and the plains,
And the pools where winter rains
Image all their roof of leaves,
Where the pine its garland weaves
Of sapless green and ivy dun
Round stems that never kiss the sun;
Where the lawns and pastures be,
And the sandhills of the sea;—
Where the melting hoar-frost wets
The daisy-star that never sets,
And wind-flowers, and violets,
Which yet join not scent to hue,
Crown the pale year weak and new;
When the night is left behind
In the deep east, dun and blind,
And the blue noon is over us,
And the multitudinous
Billows murmur at our feet,
Where the earth and ocean meet,
In the universal sun.

PERCY BYSSHE SHELLEY

The Year

The crocus, while the days are dark,
  Unfolds its saffron sheen;
At April's touch, the crudest bark
  Discovers gems of green.

Then sleep the seasons, full of might;
  While slowly swells the pod
And rounds the peach, and in the night
  The mushroom bursts the sod.

The winter comes: the frozen rut
  Is bound with silver bars;
The snow-drift heaps against the hut;
  And night is pierced with stars.

COVENTRY PATMORE

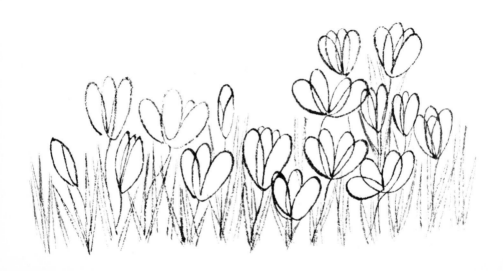

A Windy Day

This wind brings all dead things to life,
Branches that lash the air like whips
And dead leaves rolling in a hurry
Or peering in a rabbit's bury
Or trying to push down a tree;
Gates that fly open to the wind
And close again behind,
And fields that are a flowing sea
And make the cattle look like ships;
Straws glistening and stiff
Lying on air as on a shelf
And pond that leaps to leave itself;
And feathers too that rise and float,
Each feather changed into a bird,
And line-hung sheets that crack and strain;
Even the sun-greened coat,
That through so many winds has served,
The scarecrow struggles to put on again.

ANDREW YOUNG

The Thrush's Nest

Within a thick and spreading hawthorn bush
    That overhung a mole-hill large and round,
I heard from morn to morn a merry thrush
    Sing hymns to sunrise, while I drank the sound
With joy; and, often an intruding guest,
    I watched her secret toils from day to day—
How true she warped the moss to form a nest,
    And modelled it within with wood and clay;
And by and by, like heath-bells gilt with dew,
    There lay her shining eggs, as bright as flowers,
Ink-spotted over shells of greeny blue;
    And there I witnessed, in the sunny hours,
A brood of nature's minstrels chirp and fly,
Glad as that sunshine and the laughing sky.

JOHN CLARE

Clock-a-Clay

In the cowslip pips I lie,
Hidden from the buzzing fly,
While green grass beneath me lies,
Pearled with dew like fishes' eyes,
Here I lie, a clock-a-clay,
Waiting for the time of day.

While grassy forest quakes surprise,
And the wild wind sobs and sighs,
My gold home rocks as like to fall,
On its pillar green and tall;
When the pattering rain drives by
Clock-a-clay keeps warm and dry.

Day by day and night by night,
All the week I hide from sight;
In the cowslip pips I lie,
In rain and dew still warm and dry;
Day and night, and night and day,
Red, black-spotted clock-a-clay.

My home shakes in wind and showers,
Pale green pillar topped with flowers,
Bending at the wild wind's breath,
Till I touch the grass beneath;
Here I live, lone clock-a-clay,
Watching for the time of day.

JOHN CLARE

clock-a-clay—ladybird

The Eagle

He clasps the crag with crooked hands;
Close to the sun in lonely lands,
Ring'd with the azure world, he stands.

The wrinkled sea beneath him crawls;
He watches from his mountain walls,
And like a thunderbolt he falls.

ALFRED TENNYSON

The Term

A rumpled sheet
of brown paper
about the length

and apparent bulk
of a man was
rolling with the

wind slowly over
and over in
the street as

a car drove down
upon it and
crushed it to

the ground. Unlike
a man it rose
again rolling

with the wind over
and over to be as
it was before.

WILLIAM CARLOS WILLIAMS

97

New Hampshire

Children's voices in the orchard
Between the blossom- and the fruit-time:
Golden head, crimson head,
Between the green tip and the root.
Black wing, brown wing, hover over;
Twenty years and the spring is over;
To-day grieves, to-morrow grieves,
Cover me over, light-in-leaves;
Golden head, black wing,
Cling, swing,
Spring, sing,
Swing up into the apple-tree.

T. S. ELIOT

The Flower-fed Buffaloes

The flower-fed buffaloes of the spring
In the days of long ago,
Ranged where the locomotives sing
And the prairie flowers lie low:—
The tossing, blooming, perfumed grass
Is swept away by the wheat,
Wheels and wheels and wheels spin by
In the spring that still is sweet.
But the flower-fed buffaloes of the spring
Left us, long ago.
They gore no more, they bellow no more,
They trundle around the hills no more:—
With the Blackfeet, lying low,
With the Pawnees, lying low,
Lying low.

VACHEL LINDSAY

Fern Hill

Now as I was young and easy under the apple boughs
About the lilting house and happy as the grass was green,
    The night above the dingle starry,
        Time let me hail and climb
    Golden in the heydays of his eyes,
And honoured among wagons I was prince of the apple towns
And once below a time I lordly had the trees and leaves
        Trail with daisies and barley
    Down the rivers of the windfall light.

And as I was green and carefree, famous among the barns
About the happy yard and singing as the farm was home,
    In the sun that is young once only,
        Time let me play and be
    Golden in the mercy of his means,
And green and golden I was huntsman and herdsman, the calves
Sang to my horn, the foxes on the hills barked clear and cold,
        And the sabbath rang slowly
    In the pebbles of the holy streams.

All the sun long it was running, it was lovely, the hay
Fields high as the house, the tunes from the chimneys, it was air
    And playing, lovely and watery
        And fire green as grass.
    And nightly under the simple stars
As I rode to sleep the owls were bearing the farm away,
All the moon long I heard, blessed among stables, the nightjars
        Flying with the ricks, and the horses
    Flashing into the dark.

And then to awake, and the farm, like a wanderer white
With the dew, come back, the cock on his shoulder: it was all
  Shining, it was Adam and maiden,
    The sky gathered again
  And the sun grew round that very day.
So it must have been after the birth of the simple light
In the first, spinning place, the spellbound horses walking warm
    Out of the whinnying green stable
  On to the fields of praise.

And honoured among foxes and pheasants by the gay house
Under the new made clouds and happy as the heart was long,
  In the sun born over and over,
    I ran my heedless ways,
  My wishes raced through the house high hay
And nothing I cared, at my sky blue trades, that time allows
In all his tuneful turning so few and such morning songs
    Before the children green and golden
  Follow him out of grace,

Nothing I cared, in the lamb white days, that time would take me
Up to the swallow thronged loft by the shadow of my hand,
  In the moon that is always rising,
    Nor that riding to sleep
  I should hear him fly with the high fields
And wake to the farm forever fled from the childless land.
Oh as I was young and easy in the mercy of his means,
    Time held me green and dying
  Though I sang in my chains like the sea.

DYLAN THOMAS

101

I wandered lonely as a cloud

I wandered lonely as a cloud
That floats on high o'er vales and hills,
When all at once I saw a crowd,
A host, of golden daffodils;
Beside the lake, beneath the trees,
Fluttering and dancing in the breeze.

Continuous as the stars that shine
And twinkle on the milky way,
They stretched in never-ending line
Along the margin of a bay:
Ten thousand saw I at a glance,
Tossing their heads in sprightly dance.

The waves beside them danced; but they
Out-did the sparkling waves in glee:
A poet could not but be gay,
In such a jocund company:
I gazed—and gazed—but little thought
What wealth the show to me had brought:

For oft, when on my couch I lie
In vacant or in pensive mood,
They flash upon that inward eye
Which is the bliss of solitude;
And then my heart with pleasure fills,
And dances with the daffodils.

WILLIAM WORDSWORTH

Spring Quiet

Gone were but the Winter,
   Come were but the Spring,
I would go to a covert
   Where the birds sing;

Where in the whitethorn
   Singeth a thrush,
And a robin sings
   In the holly-bush.

Full of fresh scents
   Are the budding boughs
Arching high over
   A cool green house;

Full of sweet scents,
   And whispering air
Which sayeth softly:
   'We spread no snare;

'Here dwell in safety,
   Here dwell alone,
With a clear stream
   And a mossy stone.

'Here the sun shineth
   Most shadily;
Here is heard an echo
   Of the far sea
   Though far off it be.'

CHRISTINA ROSSETTI

Autumn Evening

I love to hear the autumn crows go by
And see the starnels darken down the sky;
The bleaching stack the bustling sparrow leaves,
And plops with merry note beneath the eaves.
The odd and lated pigeon bounces by,
As if a wary watching hawk was nigh,
While far and fearing nothing, high and slow,
The stranger birds to distant places go;
While short of flight the evening robin comes
To watch the maiden sweeping out the crumbs,
Nor fears the idle shout of passing boy,
But pecks about the door, and sings for joy;
Then in the hovel where the cows are fed
Finds till the morning comes a pleasant bed.

JOHN CLARE

starnels—starlings

Snow in the Suburbs

        Every branch big with it
        Bent every twig with it
    Every fork like a white web-foot;
    Every street and pavement mute:
Some flakes have lost their way, and grope back upward, when
Meeting those meandering down they turn and descend again.
    The palings are glued together like a wall,
    And there is no waft of wind with the fleecy fall.

        A sparrow enters the tree,
        Whereupon immediately
    A snow-lump thrice his own slight size
    Descends on him and showers his head and eyes.
        And overturns him,
        And near inurns him,
        And lights on a nether twig, when its brush
Starts off a volley of other lodging lumps with a rush.

        The steps are a blanched slope,
        Up which, with feeble hope,
    A black cat comes, wide-eyed and thin;
        And we take him in.

                                    THOMAS HARDY

105

To Jane

I

The keen stars were twinkling,
And the fair moon was rising among them,
   Dear Jane!
   The guitar was twinkling,
But the notes were not sweet till you sung them
   Again.

II

As the moon's soft splendour
O'er the faint cold starlight of Heaven
   Is thrown,
   So your voice most tender
To the strings without soul had then given
   Its own.

III

The stars will awaken,
Though the moon sleep a full hour later,
   To-night;
   No leaf will be shaken
Whilst the dews of your melody scatter
   Delight.

IV

Though the sound overpowers,
Sing again, with your dear voice revealing
   A tone
   Of some world far from ours,
Where music and moonlight and feeling
   Are one.

PERCY BYSSHE SHELLEY

ESCAPES

Time, you old gipsy man

Time, you old gipsy man,
　Will you not stay,
Put up your caravan
　Just for one day?

All things I'll give you
Will you be my guest,
Bells for your jennet
Of silver the best,
Goldsmiths shall beat you
A great golden ring,
Peacocks shall bow to you,
Little boys sing,
Oh, and sweet girls will
Festoon you with may,
Time, you old gipsy,
Why hasten away?
Last week in Babylon,
Last night in Rome,
Morning, and in the crush
Under Paul's dome;
Under Paul's dial
You tighten your rein—
Only a moment,
And off once again;
Off to some city
Now blind in the womb,
Off to another
Ere that's in the tomb.

Time, you old gipsy man,
　Will you not stay?
Put up your caravan
　Just for one day?　　RALPH HODGSON

Romance

When I was but thirteen or so
   I went into a golden land,
Chimborazo, Cotopaxi
   Took me by the hand.

My father died, my brother too,
   They passed like fleeting dreams.
I stood where Popocatapetl
   In the sunlight gleams.

I dimly heard the Master's voice
   And boys far-off at play,
Chimborazo, Cotopaxi
   Had stolen me away.

I walked in a great golden dream
   To and fro from school—
Shining Popocatapetl
   The dusty streets did rule.

I walked home with a gold dark boy
   And never a word I'd say,
Chimborazo, Cotopaxi
   Had taken my speech away:

I gazed entranced upon his face
   Fairer than any flower—
O shining Popocatapetl
   It was thy magic hour:

The houses, people, traffic seemed
   Thin fading dreams by day,
Chimborazo, Cotopaxi
   They had stolen my soul away!

WALTER JAMES TURNER

Old Meg

Old Meg she was a Gipsey,
   And liv'd upon the Moors;
Her bed it was the brown heath turf,
   And her house was out of doors.

Her apples were swart blackberries,
   Her currants, pods o'broom;
Her wine was dew of the wild white rose,
   Her book a churchyard tomb.

Her Brothers were the craggy hills,
   Her Sisters larchen trees;
Alone with her great family
   She liv'd as she did please.

No breakfast had she many a morn,
   No dinner many a noon,
And, 'stead of supper, she would stare
   Full hard against the moon.

But every morn, of woodbine fresh
   She made her garlanding,
And, every night, the dark glen Yew
   She wove, and she would sing.

And with her fingers, old and brown,
   She plaited Mats o' Rushes,
And gave them to the cottagers
   She met among the Bushes.

Old Meg was brave as Margaret Queen
   And tall as Amazon;
An old red blanket cloak she wore,
   A chip hat had she on.
God rest her aged bones somewhere!
   She died full long agone!

JOHN KEATS

The Gypsy

That was the top of the walk, when he said:
'Have you seen any others, any of our lot,
With apes or bears?'
                    —A brown upstanding fellow
Not like the half-castes,
                    up on the wet road near Clermont.
The wind came, and the rain,
And mist clotted about the trees in the valley,
And I'd the long ways behind me,
                    gray Arles and Biaucaire,
And he said, 'Have you seen any of our lot?'
I'd seen a lot of his lot . . .
                    ever since Rhodez,
Coming down from the fair
                    of St. John,
With caravans, but never an ape or a bear.

EZRA POUND

Winter

Snow wind-whipt to ice
   Under a hard sun:
Stream-runnels curdled hoar
   Crackle, cannot run.

Robin stark dead on twig,
   Song stiffened in it:
Fluffed feathers may not warm
   Bone-thin linnet:

Big-eyed rabbit, lost,
   Scrabbles the snow,
Searching for long-dead grass
   With frost-bit toe:

Mad-tired on the road
   Old Kelly goes;
Through crookt fingers snuffs the air
   Knife-cold in his nose.

Hunger-weak, snow-dazzled,
   Old Thomas Kelly
Thrusts his bit hands, for warmth,
   'Twixt waistcoat and belly.

RICHARD HUGHES

Nod

Softly along the road of evening,
    In a twilight dim with rose,
Wrinkled with age, and drenched with dew,
    Old Nod, the shepherd, goes.

His drowsy flock streams on before him,
    Their fleeces charged with gold,
To where the sun's last beam leans low
    On Nod the shepherd's fold.

The hedge is quick and green with brier,
    From their sand the conies creep;
And all the birds that fly in heaven
    Flock singing home to sleep.

His lambs outnumber a noon's roses,
    Yet, when night's shadows fall,
His blind old sheep-dog, Slumber-soon,
    Misses not one of all.

His are the quiet steeps of dreamland,
    The waters of no-more-pain,
His ram's bell rings 'neath an arch of stars,
    'Rest, rest, and rest again.'

WALTER DE LA MARE

The Solitary Reaper

Behold her, single in the field,
Yon solitary Highland Lass!
Reaping and singing by herself;
Stop here, or gently pass!
Alone she cuts and binds the grain,
And sings a melancholy strain;
O listen! for the Vale profound
Is overflowing with the sound.

No Nightingale did ever chaunt
More welcome notes to weary bands
Of travellers in some shady haunt,
Among Arabian sands:
A voice so thrilling ne'er was heard
In spring-time from the Cuckoo-bird,
Breaking the silence of the seas
Among the farthest Hebrides.

Will no one tell me what she sings?—
Perhaps the plaintive numbers flow
For old, unhappy, far-off things,
And battles long ago:
Or is it some more humble lay,
Familiar matter of to-day?
Some natural sorrow, loss, or pain,
That has been, and may be again?

Whate'er the theme, the Maiden sang
As if her song could have no ending;
I saw her singing at her work,
And o'er the sickle bending:—
I listened, motionless and still;
And as I mounted up the hill,
The music in my heart I bore,
Long after it was heard no more.

WILLIAM WORDSWORTH

The Listeners

'Is there anybody there?' said the Traveller,
　　Knocking on the moonlit door;
And his horse in the silence champed the grasses
　　Of the forest's ferny floor:
And a bird flew up out of the turret,
　　Above the Traveller's head:
And he smote upon the door a second time;
　　'Is there anybody there?' he said.
But no one descended to the Traveller;
　　No head from the leaf-fringed sill
Leaned over and looked into his grey eyes,
　　Where he stood perplexed and still.
But only a host of phantom listeners
　　That dwelt in the lone house then
Stood listening in the quiet of the moonlight
　　To that voice from the world of men:
Stood thronging the faint moonbeams on the dark stair,
　　That goes down to the empty hall,
Hearkening in an air stirred and shaken
　　By the lonely Traveller's call.
And he felt in his heart their strangeness,
　　Their stillness answering his cry,
While his horse moved, cropping the dark turf,
　　'Neath the starred and leafy sky;
For he suddenly smote on the door, even
　　Louder, and lifted his head:—

'Tell them I came, and no one answered,
  That I kept my word,' he said.
Never the least stir made the listeners,
  Though every word he spake
Fell echoing through the shadowiness of the still house
  From the one man left awake:
Ay, they heard his foot upon the stirrup,
  And the sound of iron on stone,
And how the silence surged softly backward,
  When the plunging hoofs were gone.

WALTER DE LA MARE

All in green went my love riding

All in green went my love riding
on a great horse of gold
into the silver dawn.

four lean hounds crouched low and smiling
the merry deer ran before.

Fleeter be they than dappled dreams
the swift sweet deer
the red rare deer.

Four red roebuck at a white water
the cruel bugle sang before.

Horn at hip went my love riding
riding the echo down
into the silver dawn.

four lean hounds crouched low and smiling
the level meadows ran before.

Softer be they than slippered sleep
the lean lithe deer
the fleet flown deer.

Four fleet does at a gold valley
the famished arrow sang before.

Bow at belt went my love riding
riding the mountain down
into the silver dawn.

four lean hounds crouched low and smiling
the sheer peaks ran before.

Paler be they than daunting death
the sleek slim deer
the tall tense deer.

Four tall stags at a green mountain
the lucky hunter sang before.

All in green went my love riding
on a great horse of gold
into the silver dawn.

four lean hounds crouched low and smiling
my heart fell dead before.

E. E. CUMMINGS

Escape

When foxes eat the last gold grape,
And the last white antelope is killed,
I shall stop fighting and escape
Into a little house I'll build.

But first I'll shrink to fairy size,
With a whisper no one understands,
Making blind moons of all your eyes,
And muddy roads of all your hands.

And you may grope for me in vain
In hollows under the mangrove root,
Or where, in apple-scented rain,
The silver wasp-nests hang like fruit.

ELINOR WYLIE

STORIES

I started early, took my dog

I started early, took my dog,
And visited the sea;
The mermaids in the basement
Came out to look at me,

And frigates in the upper floor
Extended hempen hands,
Presuming me to be a mouse
Aground, upon the sands.

But no man moved me till the tide
Went past my simple shoe,
And past my apron and my belt,
And past my bodice too,

And made as he would eat me up
As wholly as a dew
Upon a dandelion's sleeve—
And then I started too.

And he—he followed close behind;
I felt his silver heel
Upon my ankle,—then my shoes
Would overflow with pearl.

Until we met the solid town,
No man he seemed to know;
And bowing with a mighty look
At me, the sea withdrew.

EMILY DICKINSON

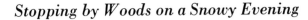

Stopping by Woods on a Snowy Evening

Whose woods these are I think I know.
His house is in the village though;
He will not see me stopping here
To watch his woods fill up with snow.

My little horse must think it queer
To stop without a farmhouse near
Between the woods and frozen lake
The darkest evening of the year.

He gives his harness bells a shake
To ask if there is some mistake.
The only other sound's the sweep
Of easy wind and downy flake.

The woods are lovely, dark and deep.
But I have promises to keep,
And miles to go before I sleep,
And miles to go before I sleep.

ROBERT FROST

The Wraggle Taggle Gipsies

There were three gipsies a-come to my door,
And downstairs ran this a-lady, O!
One sang high, and another sang low,
And the other sang, Bonny, bonny Biscay, O!

Then she pulled off her silk-finished gown
And put on hose of leather, O!
The ragged, ragged rags about our door—
She's gone with the wraggle taggle gipsies, O!

It was late last night, when my lord came home,
Enquiring for his a-lady, O!
The servants said, on every hand:
"She's gone with the wraggle taggle gipsies, O!"

"O saddle to me my milk-white steed.
Go and fetch me my pony, O!
That I may ride and seek my bride,
Who is gone with the wraggle taggle gipsies, O!"

O he rode high and he rode low,
He rode through woods and copses too,
Until he came to an open field,
And there he espied his a-lady, O!

"What makes you leave your house and land?
What makes you leave your money, O?
What makes you leave your new-wedded lord;
To go with the wraggle taggle gipsies, O!"

"What care I for my house and my land?
What care I for my money, O?
What care I for my new-wedded lord?
I'm off with the wraggle taggle gipsies, O!"

"Last night you slept on a goose-feather bed,
With the sheet turned down so bravely, O!
And to-night you'll sleep in a cold open field,
Along with the wraggle taggle gipsies, O!"

"What care I for a goose-feather bed,
With the sheet turned down so bravely, O?
For to-night I shall sleep in a cold open field,
Along with the wraggle taggle gipsies, O!"

UNKNOWN

The Happy Townland

There's many a strong farmer
Whose heart would break in two,
If he could see the townland
That we are riding to;
Boughs have their fruit and blossom
At all times of the year;
Rivers are running over
With red beer and brown beer.
An old man plays the bagpipes
In a golden and silver wood;
Queens, their eyes blue like the ice,
Are dancing in a crowd.

The little fox he murmured,
'O what of the world's bane?'
The sun was laughing sweetly,
The moon plucked at my rein;
And the little red fox murmured,
'O do not pluck at his rein,
He is riding to the townland
That is the world's bane.'

When their hearts are so high
That they would come to blows,
They unhook their heavy swords
From golden and silver boughs;
But all that are killed in battle
Awaken to life again.
It is lucky that their story
Is not known among men,
For O, the strong farmers
That would let the spade lie,
Their hearts would be like a cup
That somebody had drunk dry.

The little fox he murmured,
'O what of the world's bane?'
The sun was laughing sweetly,
The moon plucked at my rein;
But the little fox murmured,
'O do not pluck at his rein,
He is riding to the townland
That is the world's bane.'

Michael will unhook his trumpet
From a bough overhead,
And blow a little noise
When the supper has been spread.
Gabriel will come from the water
With a fish-tail, and talk
Of wonders that have happened
On wet roads where men walk,
And lift up an old horn
Of hammered silver, and drink
Till he has fallen asleep
Upon the starry brink.

The little fox he murmured,
'O what of the world's bane?'
The sun was laughing sweetly,
The moon plucked at my rein;
But the little fox murmured,
'O do not pluck at his rein,
He is riding to the townland
That is the world's bane.'

W. B. YEATS

The Way through the Woods

They shut the road through the woods
Seventy years ago.
Weather and rain have undone it again,
And now you would never know
There was once a road through the woods
Before they planted the trees.
It is underneath the coppice and heath
And the thin anemones.
Only the keeper sees
That, where the ring-dove broods,
And the badgers roll at ease,
There was once a road through the woods.

Yet, if you enter the woods
Of a summer evening late,
When the night-air cools on the trout-ringed pools
Where the otter whistles his mate,
(They fear not men in the woods,
Because they see so few.)
You will hear the beat of a horse's feet,
And the swish of a skirt in the dew,
Steadily cantering through
The misty solitudes,
As though they perfectly knew
The old lost road through the woods. . . .
But there is no road through the woods.

RUDYARD KIPLING

128

The Crescent Boat

(from *Peter Bell*)

There's something in a flying horse,
There's something in a huge balloon;
But through the clouds I'll never float
Until I have a little Boat,
Shaped like the crescent-moon.

And now I *have* a little Boat,
In shape a very crescent-moon:
Fast through the clouds my Boat can sail;
And if perchance your faith should fail,
Look up—and you shall see me soon!

The woods, my Friends, are round you roaring,
Rocking and roaring like a sea;
The noise of danger's in your ears,
And ye have all a thousand fears
Both for my little Boat and me!

Meanwhile untroubled I admire
The pointed horns of my canoe;
And, did not pity touch my breast,
To see how ye are all distrest,
Till my ribs ached, I'd laugh at you!

Away we go, my Boat and I—
Frail man ne'er sate in such another;
Whether among the winds we strive,
Or deep into the clouds we dive,
Each is contented with the other.

Away we go—and what care we
For treason, tumults, and for wars?
We are as calm in our delight
As is the crescent-moon so bright
Among the scattered stars.

Up goes my Boat among the stars
Through many a breathless field of light,
Through many a long blue field of ether,
Leaving ten thousand stars beneath her:
Up goes my little Boat so bright!

The Crab, the Scorpion, and the Bull—
We pry among them all; have shot
High o'er the red-haired race of Mars,
Covered from top to toe with scars;
Such company I like it not!

The towns in Saturn are decayed,
And melancholy Spectres throng them;—
The Pleiads, that appear to kiss
Each other in the vast abyss,
With joy I sail among them.

Swift Mercury resounds with mirth,
Great Jove is full of stately bowers;
But these, and all that they contain,
What are they to that tiny grain,
That little Earth of ours?

Then back to Earth, the dear green Earth:—
Whole ages if I here should roam,
The world for my remarks and me
Would not a whit the better be;
I've left my heart at home.

See! There she is, the matchless Earth!
There spreads the famed Pacific Ocean!
Old Andes thrusts yon craggy spear
Through the grey clouds; the Alps are here,
Like waters in commotion!

Yon tawny slip is Libya's sands;
That silver thread the river Dnieper;
And look, where clothed in brightest green
Is a sweet Isle, of isles the Queen;
Ye fairies, from all evil keep her!

And see the town where I was born!
Around those happy fields we span
In boyish gambols;—I was lost
Where I have been, but on this coast
I feel I am a man.

Never did fifty things at once
Appear so lovely, never, never;—
How tunefully the forests ring!
To hear the earth's soft murmuring
Thus could I hang forever!

WILLIAM WORDSWORTH

Kubla Khan

OR A VISION IN A DREAM

In Xanadu did Kubla Khan
A stately pleasure-dome decree:
Where Alph, the sacred river, ran
Through caverns measureless to man
   Down to a sunless sea.
So twice five miles of fertile ground
With walls and towers were girdled round:
And there were gardens bright with sinuous rills,
Where blossomed many an incense-bearing tree;
And here were forests ancient as the hills,
Enfolding sunny spots of greenery.

But oh! that deep romantic chasm which slanted
Down the green hill athwart a cedarn cover!
A savage place! as holy and enchanted
As e'er beneath a waning moon was haunted
By woman wailing for her demon-lover!
And from this cavern, with ceaseless turmoil seething,
As if this earth in fast thick pants were breathing,
A mighty fountain momently was forced:
Amid whose swift half-intermitted burst
Huge fragments vaulted like rebounding hail,
Or chaffy grain beneath the thresher's flail:
And mid these dancing rocks at once and ever
It flung up momently the sacred river.
Five miles meandering with a mazy motion
Through wood and dale the sacred river ran,
Then reached the caverns measureless to man,
And sank in tumult to a lifeless ocean:
And 'mid this tumult Kubla heard from far
Ancestral voices prophesying war!

The shadow of the dome of pleasure
Floated midway on the waves;
Where was heard the mingled measure
From the fountain and the caves.
It was a miracle of rare device,
A sunny pleasure-dome with caves of ice!

A damsel with a dulcimer
In a vision once I saw:
It was an Abyssinian maid,
And on her dulcimer she played,
Singing of Mount Abora.
Could I revive within me
Her symphony and song,
To such a deep delight 'twould win me,
That with music loud and long,
I would build that dome in air,
That sunny dome! those caves of ice!
And all who heard should see them there,
And all should cry, Beware! Beware!
His flashing eyes, his floating hair!
Weave a circle round him thrice,
And close your eyes with holy dread,
For he on honey-dew hath fed,
And drunk the milk of Paradise.

SAMUEL TAYLOR COLERIDGE

What Is Poetry?

An Afterthought

What Is Poetry?

POETRY should be a deep delight, which you would enjoy as you enjoy a day in Spring, when the sun is rising, the birds are singing, and the first flowers of the year are discovered along the edge of the woods. You must not think of it as a school subject about which you will be questioned one day; you must not even think of it as "literature" which is an ugly word invented by schoolmasters. Poetry is like the bird's song, but since it is sung by a human being, it has more meaning, and that meaning is given in words.

But the words which the poet finds—and he finds them like flowers in his path: he does not look for them—these words are special words. Some of them are sweetly musical, words that are thrilling to the tongue as we utter them; others are magical words that fill the mind with wonder. Music and magic are both present in the best poems, and together they give us the particular delight of poetry.

But that delight is not always simple delight—some poems make us sad, because they are about sorrow or death; others make us thoughtful, because they tell us what the poet thinks about life or about the many things that happen in life. Such subjects are not forbidden, but just as a clear stream will break into cloudy froth when it meets rough rocks, so thought dims the brightness of pure poetry. Poetry is not made by taking thought about a subject; rather it forms in the mind like a crystal; its words are like snowflakes that fall on a green leaf. Such an event is rare, and the perfect poems in any language are so few that they could all be included in a book much smaller than the Bible.

This book in your hands does not pretend to gather together all the perfect poems in the English language, for it is limited to those that give delight. There is a time for sadness, and there is a poetry of sadness; but this is a book of delight, and though there are a few tragic poems in it, they are poems of such magical quality that they fill us with wonder, and we feel glad that there are people who will give their lives for one another, or for the love of truth. Children are not strangers to war and death, subjects which have occasionally inspired the purest poetry; but there are many experiences which they do not share with grown-up people, and poems that describe such experiences will not be found in this book.

I have said that the delight which poetry gives us is due to its music and magic, but music and magic are inspired by what the poet *sees*—more particularly by what he sees with his "inward eye," that eye with which Wordsworth saw the dancing daffodils as he lay upon his couch (page 102). This is the eye of the imagination, and what it sees are "images"—things held in the mind as a reflection is held in a mirror. But though the outward eye has always to look at the real world to find an image, the inward eye has a private store of them. All the things we have seen in the past, and which are no longer visible, are filed away in the memory like microfilms, some near the surface, some buried so deeply that we have forgotten them. When a poet is writing, his inward eye is searching through this store of images, sweeping through it with a beam like a searchlight, and stopping immediately when he has found what he needs to illustrate his thought or feeling. Blake, in his "Laughing Song" (page 76), is searching for images in nature that suggest laughter, and his inward eye sees a dimple on the human cheek and he sees that the stream, too, is covered with such dimples. He has found an image that makes us realize how natural and delightful laughter is:

And the dimpling stream runs laughing by . . .

But the inward eye does more than pick out single images of this kind: as it roves over the memory it will see an unexpected resemblance between two separate images, and these it will pick out and combine. Two images thus brought together make a metaphor. Christina Rossetti wishes to express the gladness she feels because someone she loves has returned to her, so she takes the image of her heart and compares it with "a singing bird/Whose nest is in a watered shoot," with "an apple-tree/ Whose boughs are bent with thickset fruit," and with other images. Such metaphors often use the word "like" to make the comparison; but sometimes (and especially in modern poetry) the poet will suppress this preposition and leave it to the reader to put the images together. Francis Thompson's poem "To a Snowflake" (page 90) is a comparison of the snow crystal to a precious jewel hammered by God out of precious metal:

> Insculped and embossed,
> With His hammer of wind,
> And His graver of frost.

but the poet does not need to use the word "like." Or, to take another example, William Carlos Williams gives the whole atmosphere of Spring by putting two unusual images side by side —a red wheel-barrow glazed with rain and white chickens (page 12). It might be thought that cherry-blossom or singing birds would have been more appropriate, but images of that kind have been used thousands of times, whereas the particular shock of seeing colours so vividly after a Spring shower of rain has never been conveyed to us so effectively before. We all see such things along with all the other characteristics of Spring, but it is the poet who selects and sets apart images that ever afterwards speak for Spring.

There is something else to be said about the poet's eye—it

sees very clearly, whether inwardly or outwardly. A poet is a man who sees unusual things (or sees usual things very clearly) and then describes them very accurately.

Images also come in aid of one another. In "Kubla Khan" Coleridge wants to impress you with the power of the mighty fountain that gushed from a cavern in Xanadu (page 132). There is a direct descriptive image of huge fragments of rock being flung up by the force of the waters; and then, to re-inforce this image, the poet gives you two other images—hail rebounding as it strikes the frozen ground and chaff thrown up by the thresher's flail. All these images combine to give you a clear idea of the seething turmoil of that sacred river.

Images can do more even than this: they can make us not only see something we never saw before, or see a thing more clearly than ever before, but even make us understand something we never understood before—or never understood so clearly.

What is so important to understand, however, if you would appreciate the pure essence of poetry, is that it does not preach or argue; it deals with ideas by means of images. Poetry is not made up of words like pride and pity, or love and beauty. These are cotton-wool words—they can be squeezed into poultices or spread over wounds; they can be used to gag people's mouths or to pull over their eyes. The poet distrusts such words and always tries to use words that have a suggestion of outline and shape, and represent things seen, as clear and precise as a crystal. This does not mean that ideas should not be present in a poem (though there are poems that have no trace of an idea in them— poems like Tennyson's lines on "The Eagle"); it means that ideas are poetically expressed in images—that the poet thinks or feels in images. That is why some poems cannot be *explained* —that is to say, translated into cotton-wool words. They shimmer in the mind suggestively, like tantalizing puzzles. The two poems by Emily Dickinson, for example (pages 36 and 122) are not nonsense poems; they merely stop at the limits of meaning, waiting to give birth to ideas.

Though images are so important in poetry, poetry nevertheless is written in words, and words have sounds—outspoken sounds, or mental echoes of sounds. Poetry was originally sung or chanted, and most poetry is still singable, and could be set to music, as were the poems of Shakespeare or Ben Jonson or Campion. But since the invention of the printing press and the manufacture of books to be read by thousands of people, the habit of setting poems to music has declined, and poems are now only rarely written purposely for music. This does not mean that they should be less musical; indeed, since there is no intention of accompanying them with the notes of lutes or virginals, the words must be more musical in themselves if they are to produce a comparable effect. But just as poets see with an inward eye, so they may be said to hear with an inward ear, and they depend on the reader also listening to the poem with his inward ear.

There is a poetry that appeals to the ear mainly, as there is a poetry that appeals to the eye mainly; but there is no poetry so beautiful as that which appeals to both eye and ear, and with clear vision and sweet sound instills in us a sense of wondering delight. It is such poetry that I have tried to gather together in the pages of this book, and principally for your delight.

My purpose was not merely to give you the delight of reading poetry, but also to encourage you to write it. I have said that great poets are rare, but greatness is rare in any human activity, and to strive after it would spoil our enjoyment of life—it is better when it comes by accident, as Shakespeare's greatness did, or William Blake's. Poetry is written with enjoyment—the act of creation is one of the intensest pleasures of life. There is no reason why a child should not discover how enjoyable it is, and beautiful poems are often written by children—I have included two or three of them in this book. I hope, therefore, that children who read the poems in this book will want also to write poems. It is, indeed, more natural to write poems than to read them; and what is natural comes easy. Children do not usually write poems because grown-ups do not realize that a child *can* write poetry, and therefore they do not give them any encouragement.

It is best to begin to write poetry by writing about what you have seen. Think over the enjoyments of the day, or the enjoyments of a day long past. As the images rise in your memory, there will be a brightness about some particular incident. Describe that brightness. Or perhaps you will feel pity for a dead animal, or love for a living one—then look round with your inward eye for images that illustrate your feeling.

Or begin with words. Two or three words come into your mind, you don't know where from or why; but they seem unusual, or haunting, like a line from a song. Write them down and *go on writing*. Find words to "go with" the words that have fallen into your mind; and to help you to find words, think of the words that rhyme with the last word of the line that is haunting you. The words you think of will suggest images, and when in this manner two or three images have been born, you will begin to see the shape of a poem, and then you will be able to complete it.

Here is a poem by a boy of thirteen—one of my own children:

> White stone, crystal stone,
>> You've seen the ages pass,
> From then till now, you've seen them through
>> Those slender blades of grass.

White stone, crystal stone,
　You've seen all things go by,
You've seen the path that time did take,
　From the place where you now lie.

White stone, crystal stone,
　I leave you in the sun,
That shines on you and always will,
　For all the time to come.

A boy sees an unusual stone lying in the field—it is unusual because it is white and gleaming; it is probably a piece of quartz. He lives in a district where there are many fossils, and the great age of such stones has been explained to him, and this has impressed him. The stone he now sees is therefore for him an image of Time, but it becomes a vivid image because he has really seen that stone through slender blades of grass, a crystal shining in his path. He therefore writes about what he sees, and combines what he sees (the image) with what he feels (the passage of time). He does not worry too much about his rhymes ("come" is not a good rhyme for "sun"); but he has seen the shape of a poem, and by repeating the phrase that first came into his mind—"White stone, crystal stone"—he has given his verses a song-like refrain that binds them together.

One does not worry about the "greatness" or even the perfection of such a poem: one knows that the boy had great enjoyment in writing it, and by making us see what he saw, and telling us the thoughts that his experience called forth, he gives all who read such a poem something of the same delight.

Poetry is nothing else:

　　"This way, this way, seek delight."

CONTENTS

CONTENTS

Songs

CONTENTS

Enchantments

CONTENTS

Escapes

CONTENTS

INDEX OF FIRST LINES

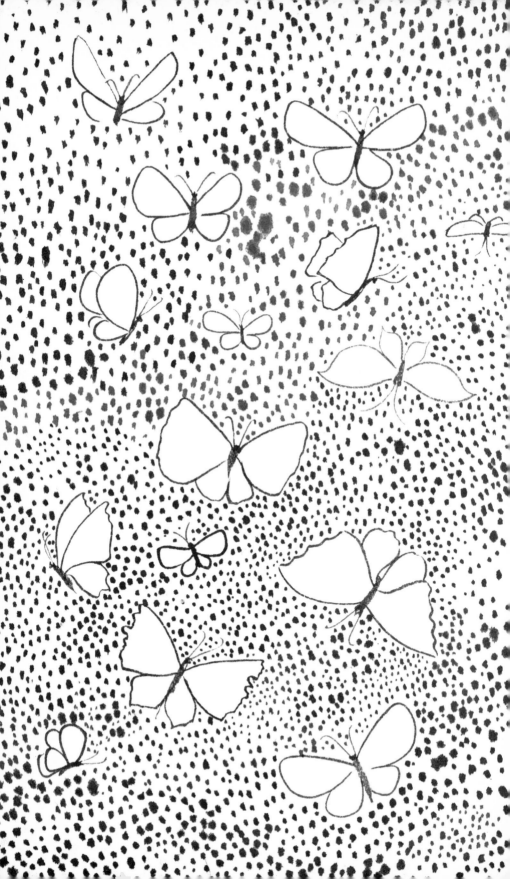

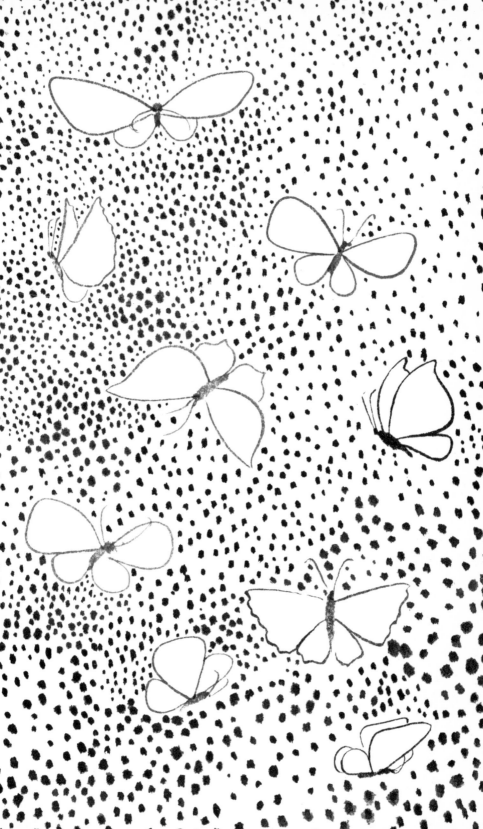